I0479115

HARRY NICK MILFORD

Launching Your Dream Business:
A Step-by-Step Guide

2023

ISBN: 9798391774280

CONTENTS

INTRODUCTION

This book aims to provide a step-by-step guide for individuals who want to start and run their own successful businesses. The book is designed to help readers navigate the challenging process of building a business, from the initial idea to execution and growth.

This book is intended for aspiring entrepreneurs who are looking for a comprehensive resource to help them turn their business idea into a profitable enterprise. It is also suitable for current business owners who are seeking strategies to improve their operations and increase their chances of success. Whether you are new to entrepreneurship or have experience running a business, this book provides valuable insights and practical advice for building a successful enterprise.

As Steve Case said, "You shouldn't focus on why you can't do something, which is what most people do. You should focus on why perhaps you can, and be one of the exceptions." Starting a business can be daunting, with numerous tasks and responsibilities to handle. However, a step-by-step guide can provide structure and organization, as noted by Brian Tracy who said, "A clear vision, backed by definite plans, gives you a tremendous feeling of confidence and personal power."

The guide breaks down the process into manageable tasks and outlines the necessary steps to complete each one. This approach can help individuals stay on track and achieve their goals. Therefore, a step-by-step guide can be a valuable resource for individuals who want to start and run their own successful business, providing a clear path to success.

This guide can help entrepreneurs plan and prepare for each stage of the business start-up process. It can help them anticipate challenges, prepare strategies to overcome them, and set realistic goals and timelines for achieving them.

Following a step-by-step guide can reduce the risk of mistakes and oversights. It ensures that important tasks are not missed or overlooked and that everything is done in the proper order. This can help entrepreneurs avoid costly mistakes that can derail their businesses.

A well-structured plan can help entrepreneurs achieve that focus and simplicity, improving efficiency and productivity. By breaking down the process into manageable tasks and outlining the necessary steps to complete each one, a structured plan can assist business owners in maintaining focus on their most critical duties and preventing time waste on unimportant ones. As Steve Jobs once said, "Focus and simplicity – once you get there, you can move mountains." This approach can help entrepreneurs accomplish more in less time and with fewer resources, ultimately leading to greater success and achievement.

This guide can also provide a framework for decision-making. As entrepreneurs encounter challenges or unexpected situations, they can refer to the guide to determine the best course of action. This can assist them in making informed decisions that align with their overall goals and objectives.

In summary, this guide can be a valuable resource for individuals who want to start and run their own successful businesses. It provides structure and organization, helps with planning and preparation, reduces the risk of mistakes, improves efficiency and productivity, and provides a framework for decision-making. By following a structured plan, entrepreneurs can increase their chances of success and build a solid foundation for their businesses.

CHAPTER 1:
CRAFTING YOUR BUSINESS CONCEPT

What do successful businesses have in common? They often begin with a unique idea that fills a gap in the market or meets an unmet need. This idea could be a new product or service, a novel way of delivering an existing product or service, or a new business model.

What makes this uniqueness so crucial? It gives the business a competitive advantage and helps it stand out from the crowd. By being different from competitors, the business can attract customers and create a loyal following. Whether you're starting a new business or looking to revamp an existing one, finding a unique idea is a critical step towards success.

Starting a business involves taking risks, and successful businesses are often willing to take calculated risks in pursuit of their goals. This may involve investing in new technology, entering new markets, or launching a new product or service. While these risks may not always pay off, the willingness to take them can lead to innovation and growth.

According to Steve Jobs, "Innovation distinguishes between a leader and a follower." Successful businesses are often committed to innovation, as noted by Jeff Bezos who said, "If you double the number of experiments you do per year, you're going to double your inventiveness." By constantly seeking ways to improve their products, services, and processes, businesses can stay relevant and competitive. The commitment to innovation can also lead to new opportunities and growth, as pointed out by Robert Noyce who said, "Innovation is everything. When you're on the forefront, you can see what the next innovation needs to be." Therefore, for businesses to succeed, they must be committed to innovation and constantly seek ways to improve.

Finally, successful businesses are often committed to excellence in everything they do. This means striving for high-quality products, exceptional customer service, and efficient operations. This commitment to excellence helps to build a strong reputation and loyal customer base, which can drive long-term success.

Identifying a viable business idea is critical for the success of any new business venture. Here are some steps you can take to help identify a viable business idea. By following these steps, you can identify a viable business idea that has the potential to succeed in the market. Remember, a successful business idea not only solves a problem or meets a need, but also has a viable market, is financially feasible, and aligns with your skills and interests.

1. Identify a Problem or Need

Look for opportunities to solve a problem or meet a need that is not currently being addressed by existing businesses or products. Think about problems or challenges that you or others face in your daily life or your industry.

Identifying a problem or need is a crucial first step in the process of developing a successful business idea. This involves looking for opportunities to solve a problem or meet a need that is not currently being addressed by existing businesses or products. This could be a gap in the market or a new innovation that addresses an unmet need.

One way to identify a problem or need is to think about the challenges you or others face in your daily life or in your industry. Consider what frustrates you or others, and think about potential solutions to these problems. For example, you might notice that there is no convenient way to transport your bicycle on a bus or train, which could lead to an idea for a new type of folding bicycle or a bike-sharing program.

It's also important to conduct market research to identify problems or needs that potential customers may have. You can gather information about people's needs and desires through various research methods such as surveys and focus groups. This can help you develop a business idea that meets a genuine demand and has the potential to be successful.

In summary, identifying a problem or need involves looking for gaps in the market or unmet needs, and considering your own experiences and those of potential customers. By focusing on solving a real problem or addressing a genuine need, you can increase the likelihood of developing a successful business idea.

2. Evaluate Your Skills and Interests

Consider your own skills, interests, and passions. What are you good at? What do you enjoy doing? Identify areas where you have a competitive advantage or expertise.

When starting a business, it's important to evaluate your own skills and interests to identify areas where you can excel. This involves assessing your strengths and weaknesses, as well as your personal interests and passions. It's essential to choose a business idea that aligns with your skills and interests because this will help you stay motivated and committed to the business in the long run.

For example, if you have experience in software development, starting a tech company may be a good fit for you. Or if you have a passion for baking, you might consider starting a bakery. By choosing a business idea that aligns with your skills and interests, you are more likely to succeed and enjoy the process of building your business.

3. Research Your Market

Once you have identified a problem or need, research your target market to determine if there is a demand for your product or service. Look for data on market size, growth potential, and competition.

Researching your market is an important step in the process of developing a successful business idea. This involves gathering information about your target market to determine if there is a demand for your product or service.

To begin, you should identify your target market - the specific group of people or businesses that you want to sell your product or service. This might involve demographic factors such as age, gender, location, or income level, or other factors such as interests or buying habits.

Once you have identified your target market, you can begin gathering data on the size and potential of the market. This might involve researching the number of potential customers in your target market, as well as their buying habits and preferences.

You should also research your competition to determine what other businesses or products are already in the market. By doing so, you can identify possible market gaps, as well as opportunities to differentiate your product or service from existing offerings.

In addition to gathering data on the market and competition, you may also want to conduct surveys or focus groups to gather feedback from potential customers. This can help you refine your business idea and ensure that you are meeting the needs of your target market.

By researching your market, you can gain a better understanding of the demand for your product or service and identify potential opportunities and challenges in the market. This information can help you make informed decisions about the viability of your business idea and develop a successful business strategy.

4. Define Your Competition

Identify your competitors and analyse their strengths, weaknesses, and market position. Look for gaps or areas of opportunity that you can leverage.

Defining your competition is an important step in the process of starting or refining a business idea. The first step is to identify your direct competitors - those who offer the same or similar products or services to the same target market. You can find competitors by searching online, attending trade shows, and talking to potential customers.

Once you have identified your competitors, it is important to analyse their strengths and weaknesses. Look at factors such as product quality, customer service, pricing, marketing, and brand reputation. This analysis will help you identify areas where your business can compete effectively and differentiate itself from competitors.

It is also important to analyse your competitors' market position. Look at factors such as market share, customer base, and geographic reach. This analysis will help you identify areas of opportunity where you can gain market share or enter new markets.

Based on your analysis of competitors, look for gaps or areas of opportunity in the market that you can leverage. These could be unmet customer needs, underserved markets, or areas where your business can differentiate itself from competitors.

Based on your analysis of competitors and the market, develop a strategy for your business. This strategy should include how you will compete effectively, differentiate yourself from competitors, and capitalize on areas of opportunity.

By defining your competition and analysing its strengths, weaknesses, and market position, you can identify areas where your business can compete effectively and differentiate itself from competitors. This will help you develop a strategy that will increase your chances of success in the market.

5. Analyse Industry Trends

Research industry trends and patterns to identify opportunities or threats that may impact your business idea. Look for emerging technologies or changes in consumer behaviour that you can leverage. Analysing industry trends is an important step when starting or refining a business idea.

The first step is to research industry trends and patterns. This can involve reading industry publications, attending trade shows, and talking to industry experts. Look for trends in areas such as technology, consumer behaviour, regulations, and competition.

Based on your research, identify opportunities that you can leverage. For example, you may identify a growing demand for a particular product or service or a new technology that can improve your business operations. These opportunities can help you refine your business idea and increase your chances of success.

It is also important to identify potential threats to your business idea. For example, you may identify increased competition, changing regulations, or shifts in consumer behaviour that could negatively impact your business. By identifying these threats early on, you can develop strategies to mitigate their impact.

Based on your analysis of industry trends, evaluate your business idea to ensure that it is aligned with current and future trends. For example, if you identify a growing demand for eco-friendly products, you may need to adjust your business idea to incorporate sustainable practices.

Industry trends can change quickly, so it is important to stay up-to-date on the latest developments. Set up alerts for industry news and regularly review your business plan to ensure that it remains aligned with current trends.

By analysing industry trends, you can identify opportunities and threats that may affect your business idea. This will help you refine your business idea and increase your chances of success in the market.

6. Test Your Idea

Before investing time and money into your business idea, test it to see if there is market demand. Consider conducting a survey, creating a prototype, or running a small pilot program.

Testing your business idea before investing time and money into it is a crucial step in the process of starting a successful business. This involves gathering feedback from potential customers, suppliers, and partners to gauge the market demand for your product or service.

One effective way to test your idea is to conduct a survey to understand the needs and preferences of your target market. This can be done through online surveys, focus groups, or one-on-one interviews. By gathering feedback from potential customers, you can refine your product or service to better meet their needs and preferences.

Another way to test your idea is to create a prototype or minimum viable product (MVP) to demonstrate the key features and benefits of your product or service. This can be done relatively quickly and cheaply and can be used to validate your idea with potential customers and investors.

Finally, you may also consider running a small pilot program to test your business idea on a smaller scale. This can help you understand the feasibility of your idea in a real-world setting, identify any challenges or obstacles that may arise, and refine your strategy based on feedback and results.

Overall, testing your business idea is an important step in validating your idea and ensuring that you are on the right track to building a successful business.

7. Consider the Financial Viability

Assess the financial viability of your business idea. Estimate the start-up costs, ongoing expenses, and revenue potential. Determine how long it will take to break even and become profitable.

Assessing the financial viability of your business idea is an essential step before starting a business. You need to have a clear idea of the start-up costs, ongoing expenses, and revenue potential. Start-up costs include expenses such as office space, equipment, inventory, and legal fees. You should also consider ongoing expenses, such as rent, utilities, salaries, and marketing costs.

To evaluate revenue potential, consider your pricing strategy, the size of your target market, and your competition. You need to determine how much revenue you can realistically generate and how long it will take to break even and become profitable.

Creating a financial plan is an important part of this step. This will help you estimate your start-up and ongoing costs and forecast your revenue and profitability. You can use financial models or hire a professional to help you create a comprehensive financial plan.

Remember, it is crucial to have a realistic view of the financial viability of your business idea. This will help you avoid financial troubles and ensure the long-term sustainability of your business.

8. Seek Feedback

Get feedback from others, including potential customers, advisors, and industry experts. Listen to their feedback and use it to refine your business idea.

The process of seeking feedback is an important step when starting or refining a business idea. Feedback can come from a variety of sources, including potential customers, advisors, and industry experts.

Knowing who your potential customers are is essential for getting relevant feedback. Depending on your business idea, you may want to seek feedback from different groups of people, such as consumers, investors, or business partners.

When seeking feedback, it is important to ask specific questions that can help you understand what people think about your business idea. Instead of asking general questions like "What do you think of my idea?" try to ask more specific questions like "Would you use this product/service?" or "What features do you think are missing?" Be prepared to listen to opinions that are different from yours. Don't take criticism personally, and try to use feedback as an opportunity to learn and improve your business idea.

Once you have received feedback, take action to implement the suggestions that you believe will improve your business idea. It is important to strike a balance between incorporating feedback and staying true to your vision for the business.

After making changes based on feedback, follow up with the people who provided it. Let them know how their feedback helped you improve your business idea, and ask for further feedback if appropriate.

By seeking feedback from others, you can gain valuable insights into your business idea and make necessary adjustments to increase its chances of success.

CHAPTER 2:
DEVELOPING YOUR BUSINESS PLAN

Do you want to start a successful business? If so, have you considered creating a well-structured business plan? A business plan is a comprehensive document that details the objectives, tactics, and financial forecasts for your enterprise. It is an essential tool that can help you stay on track as you start and grow your business. With a business plan in hand, you will have a roadmap to follow and a clear understanding of what you need to do to achieve your goals. Whether you are seeking funding from investors or simply want to keep your business on track, a well-structured business plan is essential for any entrepreneur.

A business plan provides a clear direction for the entrepreneur and the entire team. It outlines the goals and objectives of the business, the strategies that will be used to achieve those goals, and the timeline for implementation. This clarity helps to ensure that everyone is on the same page and working towards a common goal.

A business plan also identifies potential challenges that the business may face. This could include competition, market changes, regulatory issues, or financial constraints. By identifying these challenges early on, entrepreneurs can develop strategies to mitigate their impact and avoid potential pitfalls.

A well-structured business plan can also help entrepreneurs attract investors and lenders. Investors and lenders want to see a detailed plan that outlines how the business will generate revenue and achieve profitability. A strong business plan that presents a compelling case for the business's potential can help entrepreneurs secure the funding they need to get started.

A business plan can also be used as a tool for decision-making. As the business grows and evolves, entrepreneurs can refer back to the plan to ensure that they are staying on track and making decisions that align with the business's goals and objectives.

Finally, a business plan provides a benchmark for measuring the success of the business.

Entrepreneurs can use the financial projections in the plan to track their progress and determine whether they are meeting their goals.

By taking the time to develop a strong business plan, entrepreneurs can increase their chances of success and build a solid foundation for their businesses. Here are the key components of a comprehensive business plan.

1. Company Description

The company description section should provide an overview of the business, including the type of business entity (e.g., sole proprietorship, LLC, corporation), its mission statement, its history (if applicable), and the team that will be running the business.

This section should outline the legal structure of the business, which can include sole proprietorship, partnership, LLC, corporation, or any other type of legal entity. This information is crucial as it determines the tax liabilities, legal obligations, and personal liabilities of the business.

A mission statement defines the purpose and values of the business, and it should be concise and compelling. A well-crafted mission statement can help to inspire employees, customers, and investors by clarifying the goals of the business.

If the business has been in operation for some time, it may be beneficial to provide a brief history of the company. This can include milestones, significant achievements, and any challenges that the business has overcome.

This section should also introduce the key members of the business team, including their roles and responsibilities. It is essential to demonstrate that the team has the necessary skills and experience to operate the business successfully.

Overall, the company description section of a business plan is an essential component as it provides an overview of the business and its key stakeholders. It is an opportunity to introduce the business to potential investors, partners, and customers and to establish credibility and trust.

2. Market Analysis

This section should provide a detailed analysis of the target market, including the size of the market, its growth potential, and any demographic or psychographic data that is relevant to the business.

The Market Analysis section of a business plan is an essential part that provides a comprehensive analysis of the target market, which helps entrepreneurs to understand the market they are entering and how they can best position their products or services to succeed.

This section usually starts with a brief introduction of the industry in which the business operates and then focuses on the target market segment the business intends to serve. The size of the market and its growth potential are key aspects to be analysed in this section, as they help the entrepreneur to evaluate the potential demand for the business's products or services.

Moreover, demographic and psychographic data should be included in the Market Analysis section. Demographic data refers to factors such as age, gender, income, education, and occupation of the target market. Psychographic data refers to factors such as lifestyle, values, interests, and behaviour of the target market. By analysing such data, entrepreneurs can determine the needs and preferences of their target market, which will help them to tailor their products or services to meet those needs.

Other factors that may be included in the Market Analysis section are trends and patterns in the industry, competitive analysis, and barriers to entry. Understanding these factors will help entrepreneurs to identify potential opportunities and threats, as well as to develop effective marketing strategies and pricing policies for their products or services. Overall, a thorough Market Analysis is critical for any business plan and provides valuable insights that help entrepreneurs to make informed decisions and increase the chances of success for their businesses.

3. Marketing Plan

This section should outline the marketing strategy that the business will use to attract and retain customers. This may include advertising, public relations, social media, or other marketing tactics.

The marketing plan section of a business plan outlines the strategies and tactics that a business will use to promote its products or services to its target market. It is an essential component of a business plan as it helps to ensure that the business is effectively communicating its value proposition to potential customers and can ultimately lead to increased sales and revenue.

The marketing plan should start with a clear definition of the target market and customer segments. This information should be based on the research conducted in the market analysis section of the business plan. Once the target market is defined, the marketing plan should outline the specific marketing strategies that will be used to reach those customers.

The marketing plan may include a variety of tactics, such as advertising, public relations, social media, email marketing, direct mail, or events. Each tactic should be carefully chosen based on the target market and the overall marketing strategy.

The marketing plan should also outline the budget for marketing activities, including the expected cost of each tactic and the overall marketing budget. This will help to ensure that the business is allocating the appropriate resources to its marketing efforts and that the return on investment is being measured and evaluated.

Overall, a well-crafted marketing plan can help a business to build brand awareness, attract and retain customers, and ultimately drive sales and revenue growth.

4. Operations Plan

The operations plan is a section of a business plan that should outline the day-to-day operations of the business, including the production process, staffing needs, inventory management, and any other operational considerations.

It outlines the practical aspects of how a business will operate on a day-to-day basis and provides a comprehensive view of how a company will carry out its activities to achieve its objectives.

The operations plan outlines the process of creating the product or service that the business will offer. It should include details such as the equipment and technology needed for the workflow and the production capacity.

It also outlines the number of employees required to run the business and their roles and responsibilities. It should also include the required skill sets for each position and any training requirements.

The procedure for managing inventories should be also described in the operations plan, including ordering, receiving, storing, and tracking inventory levels. It should also include any methods for reducing inventory waste and spoilage.

The equipment and physical space needed to operate the business are described in the Facilities section. It should include details such as the location, lease agreements, and any necessary permits.

The operations plan also outlines the technology requirements for the business, such as software, hardware, and other technology needs.

It also lists the vendors and suppliers the company will use to get the supplies or services it needs to run.

The operations plan is critical to the success of a business because it provides a roadmap for how the business will operate, from the production process to staffing needs and inventory management. It also ensures that the business owner is prepared for any operational challenges that may arise and has contingency plans in place.

5. Financial Projections

The Financial Projections section of a business plan should include a detailed financial plan, including income statements, balance sheets, cash flow statements, and other financial data that will help investors understand the financial viability of the business. It should also include information on funding needs, such as how much money is required to start and grow the business, and how the funds will be used.

It is where the entrepreneur presents the financial details of their business. This section should provide a clear and detailed picture of the company's financial health, current and projected financial performance, and funding requirements. The financial projections typically include three primary financial statements: the income statement, the balance sheet, and the cash flow statement.

The income statement, also known as the profit and loss statement, shows the company's revenues and expenses over a period of time. It helps to determine the profitability of the business by subtracting expenses from revenues.

The balance sheet shows the company's assets, liabilities, and equity at a specific point in time. It provides a snapshot of the company's financial position and helps to determine the company's net worth.

The cash flow statement shows the cash inflows and outflows for a specific period, indicating the company's liquidity and ability to generate cash. It helps investors to understand how the company is generating and using its cash.

In addition to these financial statements, the Financial Projections section should also include information on funding needs. This may include how much money is required to start and grow the business, and how the funds will be used. This section helps investors understand the financial viability of the business and the entrepreneur's ability to manage the finances effectively.

6. The Other Sections

In addition to these key components, a business plan may also include other sections, such as a SWOT analysis, industry analysis, or competitive analysis, depending on the specific needs of the business. These are all important components of a comprehensive business plan. Here's a brief explanation of each:

1. SWOT Analysis: A SWOT analysis is a tool used to evaluate the strengths, weaknesses, opportunities, and threats facing a business. It helps entrepreneurs identify internal and external factors that may impact their business, and develop strategies to leverage strengths, address weaknesses, capitalize on opportunities, and mitigate threats.

2. Industry Analysis: An industry analysis is a comprehensive review of the industry in which the business operates. It involves analysing the market size, growth rate, trends, competition, and regulatory environment of the industry. The goal of an industry analysis is to help entrepreneurs understand the opportunities and challenges facing their business, and develop strategies to succeed in the industry.

3. Competitive Analysis: A competitive analysis is a review of the competition in the market. It involves identifying competitors, analysing their strengths and weaknesses, and evaluating their marketing strategies. The goal of a competitive analysis is to help entrepreneurs understand the competitive landscape and develop strategies to differentiate their business from competitors and gain market share.

By conducting a SWOT analysis, industry analysis, and competitive analysis, entrepreneurs can gain a deeper understanding of their business environment and develop strategies to succeed in the market. These analyses are an important part of a comprehensive business plan and are essential for making informed business decisions.

The overall goal of a business plan is to provide a clear roadmap for the business, as well as to help investors and stakeholders understand the potential for success and the risks involved in the venture.

7. Tips on How to Create a Compelling Business Plan that Will Attract Investors and Customers

Making a strong business strategy is crucial for attracting investors and clients. Here are some suggestions to assist you in writing a business plan that is distinctive:

1. Focus on the problem you are solving: Your business plan should clearly explain the problem your product or service solves and how it addresses a need in the market. Be specific about the pain points your target customers experience, and how your solution will make their lives better.

2. Be realistic with financial projections: While investors want to see that your business has the potential for growth and profitability, they also want to see realistic financial projections. Do not overinflate revenue projections or underestimate expenses. Use reliable data and market research to inform your projections.

3. Highlight your unique value proposition: Your business plan should clearly communicate what makes your product or service unique and why customers should choose you over competitors. Focus on the benefits you offer that competitors do not, and how you plan to differentiate yourself in the market.

4. Be concise and clear: Your business plan should be well-organized, easy to read, and free of unnecessary jargon. Use visuals such as charts and graphs to make complex information easier to understand. Keep the tone professional and concise, avoiding overly technical language.

5. Get feedback: Have trusted colleagues, mentors, or advisors review your business plan and provide feedback. Incorporate their suggestions and make revisions as needed to strengthen your plan.

6. Be passionate and authentic: Finally, remember that investors and customers are looking for entrepreneurs who are passionate about their business and authentic in their approach. Your business plan should reflect your enthusiasm and commitment to making your venture a success.

By following these tips, you can create a business plan that effectively communicates your vision, potential, and value proposition, and helps you attract the funding and customers you need to succeed.

CHAPTER 3:
ACQUIRING CAPITAL FOR YOUR BUSINESS

Why is financing a business important for its success? What does financing a business involve? Acquiring the necessary funds for start-up costs, operating expenses and other financial needs is essential for a business to thrive. This process, known as financing a business, involves identifying potential sources of funding and developing a financial plan to cover all associated costs.

Entrepreneurs may face challenges in obtaining financing, especially if they lack a strong credit history or collateral to secure a loan. However, there are several options available to entrepreneurs, including personal savings. Many entrepreneurs use their personal savings to finance their businesses. This can be a risky option since it may deplete personal funds, but it can also demonstrate the entrepreneur's commitment to the business.

Some entrepreneurs may turn to friends and family for financial support. This can be a less formal option, but it is important to have clear expectations and agreements in place to avoid conflicts.

Entrepreneurs can apply for a traditional bank loan, where they can borrow funds from a financial institution and repay the borrowed amount along with interest. Banks may require collateral or a strong credit history to approve a loan.

Each financing option has its own advantages and disadvantages, and entrepreneurs should carefully consider their options before making a decision. It is important to have a solid understanding of the business's financial needs and to develop a realistic financial plan to ensure the long-term success of the business.

When choosing the best financing option for their business, entrepreneurs should consider their specific needs, goals, and circumstances. Factors to consider include the amount of capital needed, the stage of the business, the entrepreneur's risk tolerance, and the level of involvement and control desired. By carefully evaluating the pros and cons of each financing option, entrepreneurs can make an informed decision about how to fund their businesses.

The most popular forms of financing are listed below.

1. Bootstrapping

Bootstrapping is the concept of starting a business with cash from personal savings or by reinvesting the revenue generated by the business. This is a common option for small businesses and startups because it enables entrepreneurs to maintain control and ownership of their businesses without the interference of external investors.

One of the advantages of bootstrapping is that it allows entrepreneurs to start their businesses without incurring debt or diluting their ownership by seeking external financing. It also helps to develop financial discipline and encourages entrepreneurs to be more resourceful in managing their businesses, as they have limited resources to work with.

However, bootstrapping can also have some drawbacks. For example, if the business requires significant upfront investments, it may be difficult for entrepreneurs to fund it entirely with personal savings. Additionally, the lack of external funding can limit the growth potential of the business, as it may not have access to the resources it needs to scale up operations or expand into new markets.

Pros:
- Maintains control and ownership of the business
- No need to give up equity
- Can be more flexible in decision-making
- Helps to develop a lean and efficient operation

Cons:
- May not provide sufficient capital for growth
- Can be difficult to manage cash flow
- This may require the entrepreneur to work without a salary for an extended period
- This can limit the ability to take advantage of opportunities

2. Angel Investors

Wealthy people who invest in start-ups in exchange for equity ownership are known as angel investors. They are often experienced entrepreneurs or businesspeople who have built successful businesses themselves and are looking to help new entrepreneurs succeed. Angel investors can provide not only funding but also valuable expertise, advice, and connections to help the start-up grow.

Angel investors are different from venture capitalists in that they typically invest smaller amounts of money, ranging from tens of thousands to a few hundred thousand dollars, and are often the first investors in a start-up. They are also usually more willing to take risks than venture capitalists, who tend to invest larger amounts of money but require a higher level of maturity and a proven track record of success before investing.

Angel investors can be found through personal networks, angel groups, or online platforms. It is important for entrepreneurs to carefully vet potential angel investors to ensure that their goals and values align with those of the start-up.

Pros:
- Can provide valuable expertise and guidance
- Can bring credibility to the business
- Provides an infusion of capital
- Can open doors to additional funding sources

Cons:

- Requires giving up a portion of ownership and control
- May have differing expectations and goals for the business
- May not have the same level of involvement and commitment as the entrepreneur
- Can be difficult to find the right investor match

3. Venture Capitalists

Venture capitalists are professional investors who typically manage large funds, with the aim of investing in companies with high growth potential. They provide capital to start-ups in exchange for equity ownership. Unlike angel investors, venture capitalists typically invest larger sums of money and often take a more hands-on approach to help the companies they invest in to grow and succeed.

Venture capitalists look for start-ups with innovative ideas, a strong business plan, and a clear path to profitability. They usually invest in companies that have already demonstrated a degree of success, such as a proven business model, a loyal customer base, or significant revenue growth.

In addition to providing funding, venture capitalists also offer strategic advice, industry connections, and other resources that can help start-ups to scale rapidly. They often sit on the boards of the companies they invest in and work closely with management teams to help them achieve their growth objectives.

While venture capital can provide a significant amount of funding to start-ups, it is a highly competitive and selective form of financing. Start-ups must have a compelling business idea, a strong team, and a clear growth strategy to attract venture capital investment.

Pros:

- Can provide significant capital to scale the business quickly
- Brings expertise and connections to help the business grow
- Can provide valuable guidance and mentorship
- Can open doors to additional funding sources

Cons:

- Requires giving up a significant portion of ownership and control
- May have differing expectations and goals for the business
- Requires a proven track record and strong growth potential
- Can be a time-consuming and complex process to secure funding

4. Crowdfunding

Crowdfunding is a form of alternative financing that allows entrepreneurs to raise funds from a large pool of investors through online platforms. The process involves creating a campaign that outlines the business idea, the funding goal, and the rewards or equity offered to investors. Rewards-based crowdfunding and equity crowdfunding are the two primary categories of crowdfunding.

Rewards-based crowdfunding involves offering backers a reward or product in exchange for their investment. For example, a company may offer a pre-order of their product or a discount on their services to backers who invest a certain amount. This type of crowdfunding is popular for small businesses and start-ups that are looking to test the market for their products or services and generate early interest.

Equity crowdfunding, on the other hand, involves offering investors equity ownership in the company in exchange for their investment. This type of crowdfunding is popular for high-growth start-ups that are looking to raise larger amounts of capital to fuel their growth. Equity crowdfunding allows companies to raise funds without giving up control of the company to investors.

While crowdfunding can be a viable option for many businesses, it requires a significant amount of effort to create a successful campaign. Businesses must have a compelling story, a clear value proposition, and a strong marketing strategy to attract investors. Additionally, businesses must be prepared to fulfil the rewards or equity promised to investors, which can be a logistical challenge.

Pros:
- Can provide access to a large pool of potential investors
- Can generate early customer engagement and feedback
- Can validate the concept and attract further investment
- May not require giving up ownership or control

Cons:
- Can be time-consuming to manage the campaign
- Requires a compelling pitch and marketing effort
- May not generate sufficient funds for larger-scale projects
- Can be difficult to stand out among other crowdfunding campaigns

5. Bank Loans

Bank loans are a common form of financing for businesses. With this option, entrepreneurs can apply for a loan from a bank or other financial institution to help fund their business. The loan amount and the interest rate depend on several factors, such as the creditworthiness of the borrower, the collateral offered, and the amount of the loan. Banks may require entrepreneurs to provide collateral, such as personal or business assets, to secure the loan. This helps to mitigate the bank's risk and provides reassurance that the borrower will repay the loan.

However, bank loans can be challenging to obtain for start-ups without a proven track record or established credit history. In such cases, lenders may require a personal guarantee from the entrepreneur or a co-signer to secure the loan. It is important for entrepreneurs to carefully consider the terms and conditions of a bank loan, including the interest rate, payment schedule, and any penalties for late or missed payments, before agreeing to borrow.

Pros:
- Provides access to capital without giving up ownership or control
- Can help build a positive credit history for the business
- Provides a set repayment schedule and interest rate

- May offer tax benefits

Cons:

- Requires collateral and a strong credit history

- May not provide sufficient capital for larger-scale projects

- Can be difficult to obtain for start-ups without a proven track record

- Requires regular loan repayments, regardless of the business's financial performance

6. Grants

Grants are non-repayable funds that are offered by various organizations, including government agencies, private foundations, and corporations, to support the growth and development of small businesses, non-profits, and other organizations. Grants are often targeted towards start-ups and entrepreneurs that meet certain criteria, such as those that focus on social impact or innovation. Unlike loans or other forms of financing, grants do not require repayment or the surrender of equity ownership in the company.

To obtain a grant, entrepreneurs typically need to submit a detailed proposal that outlines their business idea, the problem they are solving, and how the grant funds will be used. The application process for grants can be highly competitive, as there are often many applicants vying for limited funds. Start-ups that have a compelling mission, clear objectives, and a strong track record of success are more likely to be awarded a grant.

Grants can provide a valuable source of funding for start-ups, as they can help cover start-up costs, research and development expenses, and other costs associated with launching and growing a business. However, it is important for entrepreneurs to carefully evaluate the terms and conditions of any grant they apply for, as some grants may come with restrictions on how the funds can be used or may require ongoing reporting and compliance requirements.

Pros:

- Provides non-dilutive funding without repayment obligations

- Can provide access to specialized expertise or resources

- Can help build credibility for the business

- Can support social impact or innovative projects

Cons:

- Requires meeting specific criteria and eligibility requirements

- May require significant effort to apply for and secure the grant

- May not provide sufficient capital for larger-scale projects

- May require regular reporting and accountability measures

CHAPTER 4:
BUILDING A STRONG TEAM

How important is building a strong team for business success? What does a strong team consist of? Who are the right people to hire for the roles and responsibilities needed to achieve business goals? These are all important questions for entrepreneurs to consider when building a successful business. A strong team should consist of individuals with the skills and experience needed to help the business achieve its goals. It is essential to hire the best-fit candidates for each role and ensure they have clearly defined responsibilities that align with the overall business strategy.

A strong team is also characterized by effective communication, collaboration, and a shared sense of purpose. Each team member should understand their role and responsibilities within the company, and be committed to working together towards the same goals. Good communication helps to ensure that everyone is on the same page and can work together effectively.

As Henry Ford once said, "Coming together is a beginning, staying together is progress, and working together is a success." Effective communication is also emphasized by George Bernard Shaw who stated, "The single biggest problem with communication is the illusion that it has taken place." Collaboration and a shared sense of purpose are also important, as Andrew Carnegie stated, "Teamwork is the ability to work together toward a common vision. The ability to direct individual accomplishments toward organizational objectives. It is the fuel that allows common people to attain uncommon results."

In addition to hiring the right people, it is also important to provide ongoing training and development opportunities for the team to ensure they continue to grow and learn new skills. This can help to increase their motivation, job satisfaction, and productivity, which can ultimately benefit the business as a whole.

Ultimately, building a strong team takes time and effort, but it is well worth the investment. A strong team can help a business to achieve its goals, overcome challenges, and ultimately thrive in a competitive marketplace.

The following concisely expresses why developing a great team is crucial for business success.

1. Complementary Skills: A strong team should have members with a variety of skills and expertise, which complement each other. This enables the team to tackle different aspects of the business more effectively and efficiently, leading to better results.

2. Increased Creativity and Innovation: A diverse team brings different perspectives and experiences to the table, leading to more creativity and innovation. This can help the business develop new ideas, products, and services that better meet customer needs and stand out in the market.

3. Higher Motivation and Productivity: A strong team fosters a sense of shared purpose and accountability, leading to higher motivation and productivity. This can help the business achieve its goals more efficiently and with greater focus.

4. Improved Decision Making: A strong team can offer different viewpoints and opinions, leading to more informed and well-rounded decisions. This can help the business avoid pitfalls and capitalize on opportunities.

5. Better Risk Management: A strong team can help mitigate risks and identify potential challenges, allowing the business to proactively address them before they become significant problems.

Overall, a strong team is crucial for achieving business success as it can help increase creativity, productivity, and efficiency while mitigating risks and making informed decisions. Assembling the right team with complementary skills and a shared vision is an important step for any entrepreneur looking to achieve their business goals.

Recruiting, hiring, and managing employees effectively are crucial for building a strong and successful team. Here are some tips on how to do it. By following these tips, you can recruit, hire, and manage employees effectively, building a strong and successful team that can help you achieve your business goals.

1. Clearly Define Roles and Responsibilities

Before starting the recruitment process, it is important to have a clear understanding of the job positions that need to be filled, the duties and responsibilities that come with each role, and the specific skills and experience required for each position. This helps to avoid confusion and uncertainty during the recruitment process and helps to streamline the process.

When roles and responsibilities are not clearly defined, it can lead to confusion, inefficiency, and wasted time and resources during the recruitment process. It can also lead to hiring the wrong person for the job, resulting in lower productivity and higher turnover rates.

To avoid these issues, it is important to have a detailed job description for each role that outlines the tasks, responsibilities, and qualifications required for the position. This description should be reviewed and updated regularly to ensure that it accurately reflects the needs of the organization.

By having a clear understanding of the roles and responsibilities, recruiters can also identify the specific skills and experience required for each position. This helps to target the right candidates and reduce the time and effort spent on reviewing applications from unqualified candidates.

Overall, defining roles and responsibilities is a crucial step in the recruitment process as it ensures that the right people are hired for the right job, resulting in a more efficient and productive workforce.

2. Use Multiple Recruitment Channels

To attract a diverse pool of candidates, use multiple recruitment channels. Recruiters should not rely on a single recruitment channel but rather use multiple channels to reach a broader range of potential candidates. This can include traditional job boards, social media platforms, referrals from current employees or other networks, and career fairs.

Using multiple recruitment channels can help to increase the visibility of job openings and attract a larger pool of candidates, including those who may not be actively looking for a job. It also helps to increase the diversity of the candidate pool by reaching out to different demographics, backgrounds, and experiences.

Job boards are a popular and effective recruitment channel, as they allow recruiters to post job openings and reach a wide audience. Social media platforms, such as LinkedIn, Facebook, and Twitter, are also increasingly popular recruitment channels, as they provide a platform for recruiters to connect with potential candidates directly and promote job openings to their networks.

Referrals from current employees or other networks are also valuable recruitment channels, as they often result in higher-quality candidates who are already vetted by someone within the organization. Additionally, career fairs and other networking events provide opportunities for recruiters to meet potential candidates in person and build relationships with them.

Overall, using multiple recruitment channels is an important strategy for attracting a diverse and qualified pool of candidates. It helps to increase visibility and reach and provides opportunities to connect with potential candidates through a variety of channels.

3. Conduct Thorough Interviews

When recruiting candidates, it is important to conduct in-depth interviews that provide a comprehensive understanding of each candidate's skills, experience, and suitability for the job. This involves asking open-ended questions that allow the candidate to demonstrate their abilities and behavioural-based questions that help assess how they would handle different situations.

Open-ended questions are questions that require more than a yes or no answer and allow the candidate to provide more detailed responses that showcase their skills and experience. For example, instead of asking "Do you have experience in customer service?" an open-ended question could be "Can you describe a time when you went above and beyond to provide excellent customer service?"

Behavioural-based questions are designed to elicit specific examples of how the candidate has handled situations in the past, which can be a good indicator of how they would perform in a similar situation in the future. These questions often start with "Can you describe a time when..." or "Tell me about a time when..." and require the candidate to provide specific examples of their actions and behaviours.

In addition to asking questions, it is also important to actively listen to the candidate's responses and ask follow-up questions to clarify and gain more information. This helps to ensure a thorough understanding of the candidate's skills, experience, and potential fit within the organization.

Overall, conducting thorough interviews is an important step in the recruitment process as it helps to assess a candidate's suitability for the job and provides valuable information for making informed hiring decisions. Open-ended questions and behavioural-based questions are effective tools for gaining insight into a candidate's skills, experience, and potential fit within the organization.

4. Check References

As a part of the recruitment process, it is important to verify the information provided by candidates and gain insight into their work history, performance, and character. This is achieved by contacting the candidate's references, typically previous employers or colleagues, to gather information about the candidate's work experience and performance.

Reference checks are important as they provide a more complete picture of the candidate's skills, experience, and work ethic. They can help verify the information provided by the candidate during the recruitment process, such as their job title, responsibilities, and achievements. They can also provide valuable insight into the candidate's strengths, weaknesses, and working style, which can help determine whether they are a good fit for the job and the organization.

When conducting reference checks, it is important to ask specific, open-ended questions that focus on the candidate's work history, job performance, and character. This may include questions about the candidate's work ethic, communication skills, and ability to work in a team, problem-solving skills, and areas for improvement.

It is also important to ensure that the references provided by the candidate are legitimate and unbiased. This can be achieved by verifying the reference's identity, relationship to the candidate, and contact information.

Overall, checking references is an important step in the recruitment process as it provides valuable information about the candidate's work history, performance, and character. This helps to ensure that the candidate is a good fit for the job and the organization, and can help reduce the risk of making a poor hiring decision.

5. Provide Adequate Training and Support

Once you have hired employees, it is important to provide them with the necessary training and support to enable them to perform their job effectively. This involves equipping employees with the required knowledge, skills, and resources to perform their job duties, as well as providing ongoing support to help them succeed in their roles.

Providing adequate training and support is essential for employee engagement and motivation, as it helps employees to feel valued, competent, and confident in their abilities. It also helps to ensure that employees are equipped to meet the demands of their job, which can improve productivity and reduce the risk of errors or accidents.

The type and extent of training and support needed will depend on the nature of the job and the employee's level of experience. New employees may require training that is more extensive and support to familiarize themselves with the organization's culture, policies, and procedures, as well as job-specific skills and knowledge. Existing employees may require ongoing training and support to keep their skills up-to-date, learn new technologies or processes, or address areas for improvement.

Training and support can take various forms, including on-the-job training, formal classroom training, e-learning, coaching and mentoring, and performance feedback. It is important to provide a variety of training methods to accommodate different learning styles and preferences.

Overall, providing adequate training and support is critical for employee engagement, motivation, and success. It helps employees to feel valued and supported and equips them with the necessary skills and knowledge to perform their job effectively. This ultimately benefits both the employee and the organization.

6. Set Clear Performance Expectations

Employers should communicate to their employees the specific goals, objectives, and performance standards they are expected to meet in their job roles. This includes outlining the responsibilities and tasks they are accountable for, the quality of work expected, and the standards for job performance.

It is important to ensure that performance expectations are clear, measurable, achievable, relevant, and time-bound when establishing them. This provides a clear understanding of the performance objectives and allows employees to measure their progress towards achieving them.

Regular feedback is also critical to performance management. Employees need feedback to understand how they are performing, to identify areas for improvement, and to understand how their work contributes to the organization's overall success. Feedback should be constructive, specific, and timely, focusing on both strengths and areas for development.

Employers should provide regular performance evaluations to their employees, which can be used to track progress towards meeting performance goals and identify areas of strength, and areas where improvement is needed. Performance evaluations can also be used as a basis for setting goals and objectives for the upcoming performance period.

Overall, setting clear performance expectations and providing regular feedback is essential to ensuring that employees understand what is expected of them and are motivated to improve their performance. It also allows employers to track progress towards achieving business objectives and ensures that employees are meeting the standards required for the success of the organization.

7. Offer Competitive Compensation and Benefits

Employers should offer salaries and benefits packages that are in line with industry standards and attractive to potential employees. This can include salary, health insurance, retirement plans, paid time off, and other rewards and benefits.

By offering competitive compensation and benefits, employers can attract and retain top talent, and build a strong team that is motivated and engaged. Competitive compensation and benefits can also help reduce employee turnover, as employees are more likely to stay with a company that offers fair and attractive compensation packages.

When determining compensation and benefits, employers should conduct market research to determine industry standards and compare their offerings with competitors. Employers should also consider the skills and experience of the job candidates, as well as the cost of living in the area where the job is located.

In addition to traditional benefits, employers can also offer other rewards such as flexible work arrangements, remote work options, professional development opportunities, and wellness programs. These benefits can help employees feel valued and supported and can contribute to their overall job satisfaction.

Overall, offering competitive compensation and benefits is essential to attracting and retaining top talent, building a strong team, and reducing employee turnover. Employers should strive to offer fair and attractive compensation packages that meet the needs of their employees and support the success of the organization.

8. Foster a Positive Work Culture

Employers should strive to create a work environment where employees feel valued, respected, and supported. This can be achieved by promoting collaboration, open communication, and employee engagement.

A positive work culture can have a significant impact on employee motivation, productivity, and job satisfaction. It can also contribute to employee retention and the overall success of the organization.

To foster a positive work culture, employers can encourage open communication and feedback between employees and management. This can include regular meetings, surveys, and other channels for employees to share their thoughts and ideas.

Employers can also promote teamwork and collaboration by creating opportunities for employees to work together on projects and initiatives. This can foster a sense of community and shared purpose among employees.

Employee engagement can be fostered through a variety of initiatives such as professional development opportunities, wellness programs, and recognition programs. These initiatives can help employees feel valued and supported and can contribute to their overall job satisfaction.

Employers should also strive to create a work environment that is inclusive and respectful of all employees, regardless of their background or identity. This can be achieved by promoting diversity and equity in the workplace, and by addressing any issues or concerns that may arise.

Overall, fostering a positive work culture is essential to creating a supportive and productive work environment. Employers should strive to promote collaboration, open communication, and employee engagement, and to create a workplace that is inclusive and respectful of all employees.

CHAPTER 5:
CREATING A MARKETING
STRATEGY

What is marketing, and why is it important for businesses? Well, marketing involves understanding what customers want and need and then creating and promoting products or services that meet those needs. It is all about identifying your target audience and finding ways to connect with them.

However, how do you actually do this? That is where a marketing strategy comes in. This is a plan that outlines how you will reach your target audience and achieve your marketing objectives. It is like a roadmap for your marketing efforts, helping you to stay focused and achieve your goals.

As Peter Drucker, the famous management consultant, once said, "The aim of marketing is to know and understand the customer so well that the product or service fits them and sells itself."

At the heart of any successful marketing strategy is a deep understanding of your customers. What are their needs, wants, and pain points? What do they care about? By understanding your customers, you can create products or services that meet their needs and develop messaging that resonates with them.

Marketing strategies can vary depending on the business's goals, target market, and available resources. However, all successful marketing strategies share certain key components, such as a clear understanding of the target market, a unique value proposition, and effective messaging and communication.

Businesses have access to a variety of marketing channels in the current digital era, including social media, email marketing, SEO, and content marketing, among others. A successful marketing strategy should identify the most effective channels for reaching the target audience and allocate resources accordingly.

Ultimately, a successful marketing strategy should be based on data-driven decisions, flexible, and adaptable to changing market conditions and customer behaviour. By developing a successful marketing strategy, businesses can effectively promote their products or services, build brand awareness, and attract customers, leading to long-term business growth and success.

Here are some key components of a successful marketing strategy. By implementing these key components of a successful marketing strategy, you can build a strong and effective marketing plan that helps you reach your target audience, build brand awareness, and drive business growth.

1. Identifying Your Target Audience

To create effective marketing campaigns, it is essential to understand your target audience. As the marketing guru David Ogilvy once said, "The customer is not a moron; she is your wife." Identifying your target audience means understanding their needs, desires, and pain points.

Start by defining the demographic characteristics of your target audience, such as age, gender, income level, education level, and location. Next, consider their psychographic characteristics, such as values, attitudes, interests, and lifestyle. Finally, examine their behavioural characteristics, such as buying habits, brand loyalty, and decision-making processes.

As Jay Baer, a digital marketing expert, has noted, "Content is fire, social media is gasoline." By identifying your target audience, you can create targeted messaging and promotions that resonate with their needs and desires, making your content more engaging and shareable.

Moreover, understanding your target audience is crucial for allocating your marketing budget effectively. By identifying your target audience, you can focus your resources on the channels and tactics that are most likely to reach them.

In summary, identifying your target audience is the first step towards creating effective marketing campaigns that resonate with your customers and drive business growth. By identifying your target audience, you can make informed decisions about where to invest your time, money, and resources.

2. Creating a Brand Identity

Any business seeking to stand out in the marketplace and connect with consumers must have a strong brand identity. Your brand identity is a combination of visual and non-visual elements that communicate the personality, values, mission, and vision of your business.

To develop a unique brand identity, start by defining your brand personality. What words or adjectives describe your business? Are you innovative, trustworthy, reliable, or fun? Next, define your brand voice. How do you want to communicate with your customers? Are you formal, casual, or somewhere in between?

Once you have defined your brand personality and voice, you can develop the visual elements of your brand identity. This includes your logo, colour scheme, typography, and imagery. Your logo is the visual representation of your brand, so it should be simple, memorable, and reflective of your brand personality. Your colour scheme and typography should also reflect your brand personality and create a consistent look and feel across all your marketing materials.

However, creating a brand identity is not just about the visual elements. It is also about the non-visual elements, such as your mission, vision, and values. Your mission is the reason why your business exists, while your vision is the long-term goal that you are working towards. Your values are the principles that guide your business and define how you behave towards your customers, employees, and the community.

Developing a unique brand identity takes time and effort, but it is a worthwhile investment. As the marketing expert Seth Godin once said, "A brand is the set of expectations, memories, stories, and relationships that, taken together, account for a consumer's decision to choose one product or service over another." A strong brand identity helps your business stand out in the market and connect with customers, driving brand loyalty and business growth.

3. Developing a Content Marketing Plan

To elaborate on developing a content marketing plan, it is important to understand that the goal of content marketing is to provide value to your target audience. This can be achieved by creating content that informs, educates, or entertains them.

To start developing a content marketing plan, you should first identify your target audience and the types of content that would be most appealing to them. This can be done through market research, analysing customer feedback, and monitoring social media trends.

Once you have identified your target audience and the types of content they would find valuable, you can start creating a content calendar that outlines the topics, formats, and publishing schedule for your content.

In order to increase your content's visibility and audience, it is also important to ensure that it is search engine optimized. This can be achieved through keyword research, optimizing meta-tags and descriptions, and building backlinks to your content.

Overall, a well-developed content marketing plan can help establish your business as a thought leader in your industry, increase brand awareness, and ultimately drive more conversions and sales.

4. Utilizing Social Media

To elaborate on utilizing social media in your marketing strategy, it is important to understand the benefits it can offer to your business. Social media may help you engage with your audience, promote your brand, increase website traffic, and eventually boost conversions and sales.

To develop a social media strategy, you should first identify the platforms that your target audience is most active on. This can be done through market research and analysing customer behaviour. Once you have identified the platforms, you can start creating engaging content that resonates with your audience. This can include a mix of promotional content, educational content, and entertaining content.

Building a community on social media is also important for increasing engagement and loyalty. This can be achieved by responding to comments and messages, running social media contests, and collaborating with influencers and other brands.

It is important to track and analyse your social media performance to identify what is working and what is not. This can be done through social media analytics tools that provide insights on metrics such as reach, engagement, and conversion rates.

Overall, a well-developed social media strategy can help you build a strong online presence, connect with your audience, and ultimately drive business growth.

5. Utilizing Search Engine Optimization (SEO)

The process of improving your website's content and architecture through search engine optimization (SEO) will raise its placement in search engine results pages (SERPs). You want your website show up on the first page of results, ideally at the top, when consumers look up terms related to your industry. This is where SEO comes in.

To create an effective SEO strategy, you need to start with keyword research. Identify the keywords that are relevant to your business and that people are using to search for products or services like yours. Then, optimize your website's content, including headings, metadata, and alt tags, to incorporate these keywords in a natural way.

Building high-quality backlinks to your website is also an important part of an SEO strategy. Backlinks are links from other websites to yours, and they signal to search engines that your website is a trustworthy and authoritative source of information. You can build backlinks by creating valuable content that other websites will want to link to, reaching out to influencers or other websites in your industry, or guest posting on relevant blogs or websites.

Overall, an effective SEO strategy can help you increase your website's visibility, drive more traffic to your site, and ultimately attract more customers.

6. Utilizing Paid Advertising

Paid advertising can be an effective way to get your message in front of a larger audience. To utilize paid advertising effectively, it is important to develop a strategy that aligns with your marketing goals. This may include identifying the most appropriate advertising channels, such as Google Ads or social media platforms like Facebook and Instagram, and selecting the right ad format, such as display ads or sponsored content.

It is important to target your audience effectively when using paid advertising. This can be done through demographic targeting or by using customer data to create lookalike audiences. Additionally, it is important to create engaging and relevant ads that will capture the attention of your target audience and encourage them to take action.

Paid advertising can be expensive, so it is important to monitor and adjust your campaign regularly to ensure that it is achieving your desired results. This may include adjusting your targeting, ad creative, and budget to optimize your ad spending and maximize your return on investment (ROI).

7. Tips on How to Implement a Marketing Strategy that Will Attract and Retain Customers

Implementing an effective marketing strategy is crucial for attracting and retaining customers. Here are some tips to help you implement a marketing strategy that can help you achieve these goals:

1. Develop a unique value proposition: Develop a unique value proposition that sets your business apart from competitors. This can help attract and retain customers by showcasing what makes your products or services unique.

2. Create engaging content: Provide intriguing and informative material that appeals to your target audience. This can be done through infographics, films, blog entries, and social media posts.

3. Leverage social media: Use social media to connect with your target audience and promote your brand. Choose the platforms that your target audience frequents and create engaging content that encourages engagement and shares.

4. Utilize email marketing: Reaching and retaining customers is made easier with email marketing. Develop an email marketing campaign that includes engaging content and targeted messaging.

5. Utilize influencer marketing: Partner with influencers in your industry to promote your brand and reach a wider audience. This can help increase brand awareness and drive conversions.

6. Optimize your website for search engines: To improve your visibility and draw more organic traffic, optimize your website for search engines. This can include using relevant keywords, optimizing your website content, and building high-quality backlinks.

7. Monitor and measure results: Monitor and measure the success of your marketing efforts using analytics tools. Use this data to make informed decisions and refine your marketing strategy over time.

By implementing these tips, you can create a marketing strategy that attracts and retains customers, promotes your brand, and drives business growth.

CHAPTER 6:
MANAGING OPERATIONS

Effective operations management is the backbone of any successful business. It encompasses a wide range of activities and processes that are aimed at optimizing the production of goods or services, reducing costs, and improving customer satisfaction.

Operations management involves several key components, including planning, coordination, execution, monitoring and control.

Effective operations management is essential to the success of any business. It can have a positive impact on businesses in several ways, such as boosting productivity, cutting down expenses, enhancing quality, and elevating customer satisfaction. By implementing effective operations management practices, businesses can ensure that they are running efficiently and effectively and are well-positioned to compete in today's competitive marketplace.

Here are some reasons why effective operations management is important for running a successful business:

1. Efficient resource utilization: Effective operations management helps businesses optimize their resources, such as labour, materials, and equipment. This can help reduce waste, lower costs, and increase efficiency.

2. Quality control: Effective operations management helps ensure that the goods or services produced by a business meet high standards of quality. This can help improve customer satisfaction and build a positive reputation.

3. Timely delivery: Effective operations management helps ensure that goods or services are delivered to customers on time. This can help build customer trust and loyalty.

4. Innovation: Effective operations management helps businesses innovate by identifying opportunities to improve processes, products, and services. This can help businesses stay competitive and adapt to changing market conditions.

5. Risk management: Effective operations management helps businesses manage risks, such as supply chain disruptions, production delays, and quality issues. This can help minimize losses and protect the business from potential threats.

6. Scalability: Effective operations management helps businesses scale their operations as demand grows. This can help businesses expand their reach and increase profitability.

Managing inventory, supply chain, and customer service effectively are important components of operations management. By managing inventory, supply chain, and customer service effectively, you can improve your business operations, reduce costs, and enhance the customer experience. Here are some tips to help you manage these areas effectively.

1. Inventory Management

Effective inventory management is crucial for any business to optimize its operations and achieve profitability. Here are some ways in which businesses can achieve effective inventory management:

1. Utilize inventory management software: Businesses can use inventory management software to automate the ordering process and track inventory levels in real time. It also helps businesses generate reports to make informed decisions about ordering and inventory management.

2. Regularly review and update inventory levels: It is important for businesses to regularly review and update inventory levels to ensure that they have enough stock to meet customer demand without overstocking. This helps businesses avoid unnecessary costs associated with holding excessive inventory.

3. Use forecasting tools: Forecasting tools can help businesses predict demand and adjust inventory levels accordingly to avoid stockouts or overstocking. This helps businesses optimize their inventory levels and reduce costs associated with excess inventory.

4. Establish protocols for handling damaged or expired inventory: Businesses should have protocols in place for handling damaged or expired inventory to ensure that it is properly disposed of or returned to suppliers. This helps businesses avoid losses associated with holding unusable inventory.

By following these inventory management practices, businesses can optimize their inventory levels, reduce costs, and meet customer demand more effectively.

2. Supply Chain Management

The process of controlling and improving the flow of products and services from the point of production to the point of consumption is known as supply chain management. It involves all the activities required to produce and deliver a product or service, including sourcing, procurement, logistics, and distribution.

Maintaining good relationships with suppliers is important as it can lead to favourable terms and pricing. Negotiating contracts with suppliers that clearly define expectations, delivery schedules, and payment terms can help ensure that the business receives goods and services at the right time and price. Clear communication channels should also be established to ensure that any issues or concerns are addressed promptly.

Monitoring supplier performance regularly is also important to ensure that they are meeting expectations and delivering quality goods and services. This can include tracking delivery times, inspecting products for defects, and conducting audits of supplier facilities. Implementing quality control measures can help ensure that suppliers meet the necessary quality standards and can help minimize defects and waste.

Using technology such as blockchain or radio-frequency identification (RFID) can improve supply chain visibility by providing real-time tracking and monitoring of goods and services. This can help reduce the risk of fraud or counterfeit products and can help businesses identify potential issues and opportunities for improvement.

Both blockchain and RFID are technologies that can improve supply chain visibility and traceability, which can be particularly useful for businesses that deal with large volumes of goods and services.

Blockchain technology creates a decentralized and secure ledger that records all transactions and changes to data in real time. This means that everyone involved in the supply chain can have access to the same information, making it easier to track the movement of goods and services and identify any issues or inefficiencies.

RFID, on the other hand, uses radio waves to track and monitor goods and services in real time. Each item is equipped with a unique RFID tag, which can be scanned and tracked throughout the supply chain. This can help businesses to manage inventory levels, reduce the risk of theft or loss, and improve overall supply chain efficiency.

Overall, effective supply chain management is essential for ensuring the timely and cost-effective delivery of goods and services, minimizing waste and defects, and improving overall business efficiency and profitability.

3. Customer Service

Effective customer service is crucial for any business to retain its existing customers and attract new ones. The following are some ways businesses can improve their customer service:

- Train customer service representatives: Proper training can help customer service representatives provide friendly and efficient service to customers. They should be able to address customer concerns, answer questions, and handle complaints professionally and efficiently.
- Implement a system for tracking and responding to customer complaints and feedback: It is important to have a system in place to track and respond to customer complaints and feedback. This can help identify areas for improvement and prevent negative reviews or customer churn.
- Regularly gather and analyse customer feedback: Gathering and analysing customer feedback can help businesses identify areas for improvement in their products or services. This can be done through surveys, social media monitoring, or other methods.
- Use technology to enhance the customer experience: Businesses can use technology such as chatbots or automated email responses to improve response times and enhance the customer experience. This can help provide quick and efficient service to customers, increasing satisfaction and loyalty.

CHAPTER 7:
SCALING YOUR BUSINESS

Have you ever wondered what it takes for a business to grow beyond its current level of operations, revenue, and customer base? How can a business expand sustainably and reach a larger market while increasing profits? Well, the answer lies in scaling! Scaling is all about expanding a business in a sustainable way, and it often involves increasing production, expanding the workforce, entering new markets, and/or introducing new products or services.

The process of scaling can be challenging and complex, requiring careful planning and execution.

It involves assessing the current state of the business, identifying growth opportunities, and developing a strategy that will enable the business to expand while maintaining its core values and mission.

Scaling a business is not just about growing in size, but also about increasing efficiency and profitability. It requires a business to optimize its processes and operations to maximize productivity and reduce costs. This may involve investing in new technology, streamlining workflows, and improving supply chain management.

In summary, scaling a business is a crucial step in its growth and success. It involves expanding the business beyond its current capacity in a sustainable and profitable way. This requires careful planning, execution, and optimization of processes to ensure long-term success.

1. Expanding into New Markets

Expanding into new markets is a strategy that involves exploring untapped opportunities and venturing into areas that a business has not previously served. This could involve expanding into new geographic regions, both domestic and international, or targeting new customer segments that the business has not previously reached. By expanding into new markets, businesses can increase their customer base, reach new audiences, and generate additional revenue streams.

However, expanding into new markets requires a thorough analysis of the market, competition, and customer needs. A business needs to have a deep understanding of the new market, including its size, growth potential, and any cultural or legal differences. It is also essential to identify the competition and evaluate its strengths and weaknesses to determine the best approach for entering the market.

Once a business has identified a new market, it can develop a marketing and sales strategy to reach the target audience. This may involve adapting the company's products or services to meet the specific needs of the new market or creating new marketing campaigns to build brand awareness.

Expanding into new markets can be a risky endeavour, but it can also bring significant rewards for businesses that execute it successfully. By expanding their reach, businesses can diversify their revenue streams and reduce their dependence on any one market. Additionally, expanding into new markets can help a business stay competitive and remain relevant in an ever-changing business landscape.

2. Adding New Products or Services

Expanding a business by adding new products or services to its existing offerings is a strategic way to scale it. According to Jeff Bezos, the founder of Amazon, "If you're not stubborn, you'll give up on experiments too soon. And if you're not flexible, you'll pound your head against the wall and you won't see a different solution to a problem you're trying to solve." In this context, expanding into new products or services requires experimentation and flexibility to find the right solutions.

This strategy involves introducing complementary products or services that appeal to existing customers or expanding into entirely new product or service categories. By doing so, a business can diversify its revenue streams and reduce its dependence on any one product or service. This can also help to attract new customers and retain existing ones by providing more value and meeting their changing needs.

Adding new products or services requires careful market research and product development. According to Mark Zuckerberg, the founder of Facebook, "The biggest risk is not taking any risk. In a world that's changing really quickly, the only strategy that is guaranteed to fail is not taking risks." In this context, conducting market research can help a business understand the market demand for a new product or service and identify potential competitors. It is also important to develop products or services that align with the business's overall strategy and meet the needs of its target customers.

In conclusion, adding new products or services can be a lucrative strategy for a business to scale, but it requires careful planning, execution, and adaptation to market demands. Expanding a business with new products or services requires innovation, risk-taking, and a commitment to meeting the needs of customers.

3. Franchising

Franchising is a business model in which a business owner (the franchisor) licenses the rights to use their brand name, products, services, and operational procedures to another person or group (the franchisee) in exchange for a fee or ongoing royalties. The franchisee then operates their own business under the franchisor's established brand and business model, with the support and guidance of the franchisor. Franchising is a popular strategy for businesses looking to expand quickly and efficiently while minimizing financial risk.

Franchising is a tried-and-tested approach for scaling a business that has proven successful in industries like fast food or retail. Ray Kroc, the founder of McDonald's, once said, "The two most important requirements for major success are: first, being in the right place at the right time, and second, doing something about it." Franchising is a way to achieve both of these requirements as it allows a business to rapidly expand into new markets without incurring the same costs as opening new locations or hiring new employees.

The benefits of franchising include greater brand recognition, wider market penetration, and reduced costs. However, it is crucial to select the right franchisees and train them to ensure they are a good fit for the business. Franchisees who understand the business's products and customers and share the same passion for success can help to ensure that the franchising relationship is successful. Furthermore, establishing a detailed franchising agreement can help to ensure that the franchisor's and franchisee's rights and responsibilities are clear and mutually beneficial.

4. Strategic Partnerships

Strategic partnerships refer to the collaboration between two or more businesses to achieve a common goal or objective. In the context of scaling a business, a strategic partnership is a mutually beneficial arrangement between two businesses that brings about advantages such as access to new markets, expertise, and resources.

Partnering with complementary businesses allows a company to leverage the strengths of each partner to achieve shared goals. For example, a business that specializes in software development may partner with a company that specializes in hardware development to create a new product that incorporates both elements.

Collaborating on joint marketing initiatives can also be an effective way to reach new customers and increase sales. For instance, a clothing retailer might team up with a popular social media influencer to showcase their products to a wider audience.

Co-developing new products or services with other businesses can also help to diversify a company's offerings and expand its market reach. This could involve partnering with suppliers or manufacturers to create exclusive products or collaborating with other businesses to develop new services that complement each other's offerings.

Overall, forming strategic partnerships can be an effective strategy for scaling a business by accessing new resources, expertise, and markets that might not be otherwise available.

5. Technology

Leveraging technology can be a powerful tool for businesses looking to scale. By automating processes, businesses can increase efficiency and reduce costs, which can free up resources for growth. For example, a business may implement software to automate repetitive tasks, such as invoicing or inventory management. This can reduce the workload for employees and allow them to focus on higher-value tasks.

Implementing new software or tools can also help businesses improve efficiency and streamline operations. For example, a business may use a project management tool to track tasks and deadlines, or a customer relationship management (CRM) system to manage customer interactions and sales leads. These tools can help businesses stay organized and better serve their customers.

Finally, using data analytics can help businesses optimize their operations and make more informed decisions. By analysing data from various sources, such as sales data or customer feedback, businesses can identify trends and patterns that can inform their strategy. This can help businesses make decisions about product development, marketing campaigns, and resource allocation.

Overall, leveraging technology can be an effective strategy for scaling a business. However, it is important for businesses to carefully evaluate their needs and choose the right technology solutions for their specific situation.

6. Tips on How to Scale Your Business while Maintaining Its Core Values and Mission

Maintaining core values and mission is critical when scaling a business. Here are some tips to help you scale your business. By following these tips, you can scale your business while staying true to its core values and mission. This can help you build a strong and sustainable business that is aligned with your vision and values.

1. Develop a clear vision and strategy: Having a clear vision and strategy for your business can help you stay focused on your core values and mission as you scale. Your vision and strategy should be aligned with your mission and should guide all your decisions as you grow your business.

2. Hire the right people: Hiring employees who share your core values and mission can help ensure that these values are ingrained in your company culture as you scale. Make sure to establish a clear hiring process that evaluates candidates based on their fit with your culture.

3. Communicate effectively: Effective communication is crucial when scaling a business while maintaining core values and mission. Communicate your values and mission clearly to your employees, customers, and stakeholders. Make sure that everyone in your organization understands the importance of these values and is committed to upholding them.

4. Monitor performance: Monitoring performance can help you ensure that your business is staying true to its core values and mission as it scales. Establish key performance indicators (KPIs) that measure the impact of your values and mission, and track these metrics regularly.

5. Be flexible: Being flexible and adaptable is important when scaling a business. As your business grows, you may need to adjust your strategy and operations to maintain your core values and mission. Be open to change and willing to pivot as needed to stay aligned with your vision and values.

CHAPTER 8:
MANAGING FINANCES

Why is managing the financial aspect of a business important? The financial aspect of a business is vital to its long-term success. Why? Managing finances ensures that a business has enough money to cover expenses, invest in growth, and generate profits. Proper financial management is crucial to the survival of a business, as it enables the company to pay bills, make investments, and plan for the future. Without proper management of finances, a business may struggle to stay afloat, grow or even survive.

Warren Buffet, a well-known businessman, investor, and philanthropist, once said, "Accounting is the language of business." Understanding financial statements is crucial to make sound business decisions. Financial statements and metrics, such as gross margin, net profit margin, and return on investment (ROI), provide insight into a business's financial health and performance. As Dave Ramsey, a personal finance expert, said, "A budget is telling your money where to go instead of wondering where it went." Creating and sticking to a budget is essential to managing finances effectively.

Managing cash flow is crucial to ensure there is enough money to cover expenses and invest in growth. Keeping track of cash flow is essential to monitor a business's financial health and make necessary adjustments to ensure long-term success.

Understanding financial statements and metrics is a key component of managing the financial aspect of a business. Financial statements including the balance sheet, income statement, and cash flow statement reveal a company's financial health and performance. Metrics such as gross margin, net profit margin, and return on investment (ROI) help business owners and managers make informed decisions about investments, expenses, and pricing strategies.

1. Creating a Budget and Managing Cash Flow

Creating a budget is a vital aspect of managing the financial aspect of a business. A budget serves as a financial plan that outlines the expected income and expenses over a specific period. It helps businesses to allocate resources effectively, prioritize spending, and make informed financial decisions.

There are different types of budgets that businesses can create, such as sales budgets, expense budgets, and cash budgets. Sales budgets focus on projecting future sales revenue, while expense budgets focus on anticipated expenses. A cash budget helps businesses to manage their cash flow effectively by tracking the inflow and outflow of cash over a specific period.

Cash flow management is another essential aspect of managing a business's finances. It involves monitoring the amount of cash flowing in and out of the business to ensure there is always enough to cover expenses. By monitoring cash flow, businesses can identify potential cash shortages and take proactive measures to avoid financial difficulties.

Creating a budget involves several steps, including identifying and estimating revenue sources, forecasting expenses, and setting financial goals. It is essential to involve all stakeholders in the budget creation process, including managers, employees, and financial advisors.

Overall, creating and managing a budget is critical for a business's long-term success. It helps businesses to plan ahead, make informed financial decisions, and allocate resources effectively.

2. Minimizing Expenses and Maximizing Profits

Minimizing expenses and maximizing profits are essential components of managing the financial aspect of a business. By reducing expenses and increasing revenue, businesses can improve their bottom line and ensure long-term financial stability. There are several strategies that businesses can employ to minimize expenses and maximize profits.

Negotiating with suppliers is one strategy that businesses can use to reduce expenses. By negotiating lower prices for raw materials, products, or services, businesses can reduce their cost of goods sold (COGS) and increase their profit margins. This can involve negotiating long-term contracts or bulk purchasing to secure favourable pricing terms.

Outsourcing certain tasks is another strategy that businesses can use to minimize expenses. Outsourcing can include outsourcing accounting, marketing, or IT services to specialized firms. This can help businesses reduce their overhead costs, such as salaries and benefits, as well as gain access to specialized expertise and technology.

Increasing sales revenue is also crucial for maximizing profits. This can involve expanding marketing efforts to reach new customers, improving customer service to increase customer retention, and introducing new products or services to existing customers. Additionally, businesses can optimize their pricing strategy to ensure they are maximizing profit margins while remaining competitive in the marketplace.

Overall, minimizing expenses and maximizing profits requires a careful balance between cost-cutting and revenue growth. Businesses must ensure that they are not sacrificing quality or customer satisfaction in their pursuit of profit. Additionally, businesses should regularly monitor and adjust their expenses and revenue to ensure they are on track to achieve their financial goals.

3. Securing and Managing Business Loans

Obtaining a business loan is a common way for entrepreneurs to secure the necessary funds to start or grow their businesses. There are various options available for securing business loans, and each has its own requirements and qualifications.

Traditional bank loans are a common option for businesses that have a solid credit history and collateral to offer. Bank loans can be used for a variety of business purposes, such as purchasing equipment or real estate, expanding operations, or increasing working capital. However, the application process for bank loans can be lengthy and involved, and the requirements for collateral and creditworthiness can be strict.

Crowdfunding is a newer option for businesses to raise funds from a large group of people, typically through online platforms. Crowdfunding campaigns can be used to fund a variety of business activities, such as product development or marketing initiatives. However, it requires careful planning and execution, as well as a strong marketing strategy to attract potential investors.

Once a loan has been secured, it is important to manage it properly to ensure that the business can meet the repayment terms. This may involve developing a budget and cash flow projection, monitoring expenses, and making payments on time. Strategies for managing debt can include consolidating loans or renegotiating payment terms to reduce monthly payments or lower interest rates.

Additionally, it is important to maintain a good relationship with the lender and communicate any changes or issues that may affect the business's ability to repay the loan. This can help to prevent default or foreclosure and maintain a positive credit rating.

For traditional bank loans, the requirements and qualifications may vary depending on the lender and the type of loan. Generally, lenders will require a detailed business plan, financial statements, and collateral or personal guarantees to secure the loan. It is important to shop around and compare loan options to find the best terms and interest rates.

Overall, securing and managing business loans is an important aspect of financial management for businesses of all sizes. By understanding the different options available and developing a sound repayment strategy, businesses can secure the necessary funds to achieve their growth and expansion goals.

4. Understanding Financial Statements and Metrics

Financial statements are key documents that provide information about a company's financial performance and position. The three main types of financial statements are the income statement, balance sheet, and cash flow statement.

The income statement is a financial statement that gives an overview of a company's earnings and costs for a given time period, usually a quarter or a year. Because it reveals whether the company has made a profit or a loss during the time under review, the income statement is also frequently referred to as the profit and loss statement.

The income statement begins with the company's total revenue, which is the amount of money it earned from selling its products or services. The cost of items sold is subtracted from this to determine the gross profit. The direct costs, such as labour and materials, involved in creating and providing the goods or services are included in the cost of goods sold.

Next, the income statement lists the company's operating expenses, such as rent, utilities, salaries, and marketing expenses. These expenses are deducted from the gross profit to arrive at the operating profit. Operating profit represents the profit or loss generated by the company's normal business operations.

After deducting interest and taxes, the income statement arrives at the company's net income or loss. If the net income is positive, it indicates that the company made a profit during the period. If the net income is negative, it indicates that the company suffered a loss.

Overall, the income statement is a valuable tool for analysing a company's financial health and profitability. It can help business owners and investors make informed decisions about how to allocate resources and grow the business.

The balance sheet is a financial statement that provides a snapshot of a company's financial position at a particular point in time, usually at the end of an accounting period, such as a month or a year. It presents the company's assets, liabilities, and equity, and shows how these three components are related to each other.

Assets are resources that a company has ownership and control over, which are anticipated to yield economic benefits in the future. They are listed in order of their liquidity, meaning how quickly they can be converted into cash. Cash, accounts receivable, stock, real estate, machines and appliances, and investments are a few examples of assets.

Liabilities are the company's obligations to pay debts or provide goods and services in the future. They are also listed in order of their maturity or when they are due to be paid. Examples of liabilities include accounts payable, loans payable, salaries payable, and taxes payable.

When liabilities are subtracted, equity is the company's remaining interest in its assets. It includes the funds invested by shareholders, retained earnings, and other comprehensive income.

The balance sheet is an important instrument for evaluating the stability and health of a company's finances. It is used to calculate important financial ratios such as the debt-to-equity ratio, which compares a company's debt to its equity and helps determine the company's overall leverage. By analysing the balance sheet, investors, creditors, and analysts can gain insight into a company's liquidity, solvency, and financial strength.

The cash flow statement is a type of financial statement that shows how much money comes in and goes out of a business over a given period of time. This statement's goal is to provide light on the company's liquidity and ability to pay its immediate financial obligations.

Operating activities, investing activities, and financing activities make up the three sections of the statement. The cash flows from a company's main business activities, such as sales, purchases, and expenses, are displayed in the operating activities section. The cash flows associated with investments in assets like property, plant, and equipment are displayed in the section on investing activities. The cash flows linked to the company's financing activities, such as issuing or repurchasing stock, paying dividends, and receiving or repaying loans, are shown in the financing activities section.

The cash flow statement can help investors and analysts to better understand a company's financial health and its ability to generate cash. Positive cash flows from operations indicate that a company is generating cash from its core business activities, which is generally seen as a good sign. Negative cash flows from operations may indicate that a company is struggling to generate cash from its core business activities.

Additionally, the cash flow statement can help identify potential liquidity issues. It is possible, for instance, for a business to have positive net income on the income statement yet negative cash flow from operating activities on the cash flow statement. This could indicate that the company is using non-cash items such as depreciation to boost its net income, but is struggling to generate cash from its operations.

When analysing financial statements, there are several key metrics to look for. These include revenue growth, gross profit margin, operating profit margin, net profit margin, return on equity, and debt-to-equity ratio. Understanding these metrics and how they relate to each other can provide valuable insights into a company's financial health and performance.

Here is an overview of each of the key financial metrics:

Revenue growth: This metric shows the rate at which a company's revenue is increasing over time. Positive revenue growth is generally seen as a good sign that a company is expanding and increasing its market share.

Gross profit margin: The percentage of revenue that is still available after deducting the cost of products sold is represented by this metric. A higher gross profit margin shows that a business can make money from its goods or services.

Operating profit margin: This metric shows the percentage of revenue that remains after deducting operating expenses, such as salaries, rent, and utilities. A company's ability to effectively manage its costs is demonstrated by a higher operating profit margin.

Net profit margin: This metric displays the percentage of revenue that is still available after all costs, including taxes and interest, have been paid. A higher net profit margin shows that a business may be profitable even after all costs are deducted.

Return on equity (ROE): This metric shows the rate of return that a company is able to generate on the equity invested by shareholders. A higher ROE indicates that a company is efficient at generating profits from the capital invested by shareholders.

Debt-to-equity ratio: This metric reveals how much of a company's funding is provided by debt as opposed to equity. A higher debt-to-equity ratio shows that a business is more dependent on borrowing money to fund its operations. High levels of debt can increase a company's financial risk, as it may be difficult to repay debt in the event of financial difficulty.

It is important to note that these metrics should be analysed in conjunction with each other, as a company may have strong performance in one area but weaker performance in another.

CONCLUDING REMARKS

We covered various topics related to starting and scaling a successful business. Overall, this book provides a comprehensive guide on starting and scaling a successful business, covering various topics such as idea validation, business planning, financing, team building, marketing, operations management, and scaling strategies.

Do you have a passion for entrepreneurship and a desire to build a successful business? Are you tired of just dreaming about it and ready to take action?

If you have a dream of starting your own successful business, now is the time to take action and turn that dream into a reality. The insights and tips shared above can help you identify a viable business idea, validate it through market research, develop a compelling business plan, secure financing, build a strong team, implement effective marketing strategies, and manage operations while scaling your business. Remember, building a successful business requires hard work, determination, and persistence, but the rewards can be immense. So, do not wait any longer, take action today and start building the business of your dreams.

As Steve Jobs said, "Your work is going to fill a large part of your life, and the only way to be truly satisfied is to do what you believe is great work. And the only way to do great work is to love what you do. If you have not found it yet, keep looking. Do not settle. As with all matters of the heart, you'll know when you find it." If starting your own business is what you believe is great work, then there is no better time than now to start pursuing that dream.

But where do you start? How do you identify a viable business idea and turn it into a profitable venture? The tips and insights shared above can guide you through the process of validating your idea, developing a business plan, securing financing, and building a strong team to help you scale your business.

However, as Colin Powell once said, "A dream doesn't become reality through magic; it takes sweat, determination and hard work." Building a successful business requires a lot of hard work, dedication, and persistence. It will not happen overnight, but with the right mindset and a willingness to put in the effort, you can achieve your goals.

So what are you waiting for? Take the first step today and start building the business of your dreams. As Walt Disney said, "All our dreams can come true, if we have the courage to pursue them." Good luck on your journey!

☙

The illustrations used in this project are sourced from PxHere.com, and are licensed under CC0 Public Domain, making them free for personal and commercial use.